CAMBRIDGE
UNIVERSITY PRESS

UNIVERSITY *of* CAMBRIDGE
ESOL Examinations

D1681080

Cambridge English

Objective
First for Schools

Practice test booklet
without answers

Helen Chilton **Helen Tiliouine**

Third Edition

CAMBRIDGE
UNIVERSITY PRESS

University Printing House, Cambridge CB2 8BS, United Kingdom

Cambridge University Press is part of the University of Cambridge.

It furthers the University's mission by disseminating knowledge in the pursuit of education, learning and research at the highest international levels of excellence.

www.cambridge.org
Information on this title: www.cambridge.org

© Cambridge University Press 2012

This publication is in copyright. Subject to statutory exception and to the provisions of relevant collective licensing agreements, no reproduction of any part may take place without the written permission of Cambridge University Press.

First published 2012
5th printing 2014

Printed in the United Kingdom by Latimer Trend

A catalogue record for this publication is available from the British Library

ISBN 978-0-521-178785 Student's Book without answers with CD-ROM
ISBN 978-0-521-178792 Student's Book with answers with CD-ROM
ISBN 978-0-521-179096 Teacher's Book with Teacher's Resources Audio CD/CD-ROM
ISBN 978-0-521-178815 Class Audio CDs (2)
ISBN 978-0-521-178808 Workbook without answers with Audio CD
ISBN 978-0-521-178822 Workbook with answers with Audio CD
ISBN 978-0-521-178839 Student's Book Pack (Student's Book with answers with CD-ROM and Class Audio CDs)
ISBN 978-1-107-648913 For Schools Practice Test Booklet with answers with Audio CD
ISBN 978-1-107-648920 For Schools Practice Test Booklet without answers
ISBN 978-1-107-602489 For Schools Pack (Student's Book and Practice Test Booklet without answers with Audio CD)

Additional resources for this publication at www.cambridge.org/objectivefirst

Cambridge University Press has no responsibility for the persistence or accuracy of URLs for external or third-party internet websites referred to in this publication, and does not guarantee that any content on such websites is, or will remain, accurate or appropriate. Information regarding prices, travel timetables, and other factual information given in this work is correct at the time of first printing but Cambridge University Press does not guarantee the accuracy of such information thereafter.

Produced by eMC Design Ltd

Contents

Answers and recording scripts
(These can be found on the Teacher's Resources Audio CD/CD-ROM)

Acknowledgements

The authors and publishers acknowledge the following sources of copyright material and are grateful for the permissions granted. While every effort has been made, it has not always been possible to identify the sources of all the material used, or to trace all copyright holders. If any omissions are brought to our notice, we will be happy to include the appropriate acknowledgements on reprinting.

Cambridge ESOL or the FCEfs 'Can DO Summary' on p. 5. Reproduced with permission of Cambridge ESOL;

The Daily Record for the text on p. 6 adapted from 'The circus school where classes include fire-eating and the trapeze' by Brian McIver, Daily Record, July 2009, © Scottish Daily Record & Sunday Mail Ltd.

Photo acknolwledgements:
p. 8: © Paul Glendell / Alamy; p. 11 (TL): © Inmagine; p. 11 (TR): © Myrleen Pearson / Alamy; p. 11 (BL): © Jack Hollingsworth / Photodisc / Thinkstock; p. 11 (BR): © Radius Images / Alamy; p. 14: © Bryan Busovicki / Shutterstock; p. 16: © Stephen Frink / Alamy; p. 24: © Nivek Neslo / Getty Images; p. 30: © Timothy Large / Shutterstock; p. 36: © Alejandro Rivera / iStockphoto; p. 38: © Stayer / Shutterstock.com; p. 45: © Petrenko / Shutterstock; p. 46: © Kalle Singer / Getty Images; p. 49 (T): © Alex Segre / Alamy; p. 49 (B): © Holger Burmeister / Alamy; p. 50 (T): © Matt Fagg / Alamy; p. 50 (B): © Image Source / Getty Images; p. 51 (TL): © BananaStock / Thinkstock; p. 51 (TR): Arkadiusz Komski / Shutterstock; p. 51 (CL): ©Janine Wiedel Photolibrary / Alamy; p. 51 (CR): © Peter Roos / Photolibrary; p. 51 (BL): © Peter Mason / Getty Images; p. 51 (BR): © Jaime Duplass / Shutterstock; p. 52 (T): © JGI / Getty Images; p. 52 (B): © Stephen Morris / iStockphoto; p. 53 (T): © Coll-Kwame Zikomo / Photolibrary; p. 53 (B): © iofoto / Shutterstock; p. 54 (TL): © John Terence Turner / Getty Images; p. 54 (TR): © 1MoreCreative / iStockphoto; p. 54 (CL): © omgimages / iStockphoto; p. 54 (CR): © John Powell / Photolibrary; p. 54 (BL): © Donald Gargano / Shutterstock; p. 54 (BR): © Kim Karpeles / Alamy.

Author acknowledgements:
The authors would like to thank Joanne Hunter for editorial support, Annette Capel and Wendy Sharp for all their help and good advice

Helen Tiliouine would like to thank Adam and Oliver for inside knowledge and Ahmed for all the cooking.

Helen Chilton would also like to thank her niece, Ellie, for her help and ideas.

Picture research by Emma O'Neill.

Audio recordings by Dsound.

Introduction

This booklet contains two complete practice tests for the Cambridge English: First for Schools exam. The tests cover topics typically included in the exam and also target the content of *Objective First* Student's Book. Students can use these tests on their own or with a teacher.

Cambridge English: First for Schools is a new version of the First Certificate exam for candidates between the ages of 12 and 15. First for Schools has the same format and task types as First Certificate, and the level of the two versions is identical, but the content and topics are dealt with in ways which reflect the experiences and interests of younger candidates.

First Certificate is at level B2 of the Council of Europe Common European Framework of Reference (CEFR) for Languages. The following 'Can Do' statements show what language learners at First Certificate (B2) level are generally able to do.

Typical abilities	Listening and Speaking	Reading and Writing
Overall general ability	CAN identify the expression of feelings and attitudes such as criticism, disapproval, agreement, and so on. CAN start, have and end conversations on familiar topics.	CAN express views, feelings and opinions effectively in writing, and give reasons. CAN find relevant information in texts.
Social and Leisure	CAN follow TV programmes and films if they are spoken at a normal speed and in standard English. CAN understand and discuss the stories in films, books and TV programmes with his/her friends.	CAN write emails and letters which are more or less formal, according to how well he/she knows the person he/she is writing to (for example, to get information he/she needs for a school project or about a social activity). CAN write about events and experiences in a detailed and readable way.
School and Study	CAN ask for factual information and understand the answer. CAN ask for clarification and further explanation and will probably understand the answer.	CAN write essays on topics he/she has clear opinions about, and present his/her argument. CAN read and understand factual texts on topics he/she is not familiar with, if he/she can use a dictionary. CAN make simple notes for study purposes, capturing the most important points.

The First for Schools examination is part of the Cambridge ESOL Main Suite examinations, which cover CEFR levels A2 to C2. The following table demonstrates how the five Main Suite examinations correlate to the CEFR levels.

Proficiency (CPE)	C2 Mastery
Advanced (CAE)	C1 Effective proficiency
First (FCE)	B2 Vantage
Preliminary (PET)	B1 Threshold
Key (KET)	A2 Waystage

The First Certificate / First for Schools examination is an upper-intermediate exam in English and can also be a first step for those wishing to progress towards the Cambridge English: Advanced exam and other Cambridge ESOL examinations.

Good luck with these tests, and with First for Schools!

Test 1
Paper 1 (1 hour)
Reading Part 1

Questions 1 – 8

You are going to read a magazine article by a teenage reporter, about a day he spent learning circus skills. For questions **1 – 8**, choose the answer (**A**, **B**, **C** or **D**) which you think fits best according to the text.
Mark your answers **on the separate answer sheet**.

Circus school for a day

Hanging upside down from the high roof attached to a set of ropes, the blood rushing to my head was the least of my worries. Five metres off the ground, the cords around my waist started to loosen. I could feel myself slipping and grabbed on to the rope with one hand to stop myself crashing down, before I was lowered to the floor. But as I landed, a hook caught my T-shirt and it was nearly pulled off. Five minutes into my training for the circus ring, and surrounded by performers laughing at me, I was already feeling rather silly. And that clumsy start made me all the more nervous about attempting fire-eating later in the day.

It is said that to succeed in the circus, what you primarily need is a lack of fear, with endless enthusiasm coming a close second. By teaching me fire-eating, circus specialist
15 Bryan planned to help me with this. Bryan said the key to the trick was not to breathe in. If you do, you risk sucking the flames inside you and burning your lungs. I could hardly bear to watch him demonstrate. Then it was my turn – I lowered the flames towards my mouth, and although I looked like I was eating something that had been left on a barbecue for too long, I was ready. The flames got lower and lower, and as a small spark fell and burnt my T-shirt, my fear, or common sense, got the better of me and I had to pull away. Although I did get the fire to within a few millimetres of my mouth, I thought I'd leave it to the experts.

I reckoned I had already proved how bold I was when another instructor, Nick, took me through the art of the bungee trapeze. This involves having two elastic bungee ropes tied to either side of you, so you can bounce up and down. To go head over heels and turn a 360-degree somersault, you push back and lift your legs up, and once upside down, lift your head up to get your body upright again. I went for the full 360-degree turn, and after a moment when I thought I'd be stuck upside down forever,

I got all the way around in one go, then was hooked, eventually managing three somersaults in a row.

For my next trick, it was back to the high-wire work, and trapeze expert Moira had to teach me the basics. Moira showed me how it was done as she pulled and swung herself up from the ground onto the trapeze swing in a move that could not have looked smoother or easier if she had been born on a swinging trapeze. Using her hands to grab the bar, she swung her legs up and pulled herself onto it within seconds.

But then it was my turn. With the bar hanging two metres above the ground, climbing it proved a bit of a challenge, but with Moira's help I did and then was very disappointed when I realised that wasn't the trick itself, it was only the starting point. The first trick involved leaning to one side, holding yourself with one hand on the rope and lying elegantly flat and extended. There was nothing elegant, flat or extended about my attempt, so we moved on to the second trick, the standing star. You stand upright on the bar, push one foot into one of the side ropes, then lift yourself up by your arms to put the other foot onto the other rope, extend the arms and wait for the audience to bring the house down, if that's what you deserve. I don't 57 think my performance would have got such a response in an actual show; I'd have to do a bit more practice first!

So after one day of circus school and clowning, I was pleased to have survived, and asked Nick how he thought I had done. 'You showed you were very keen and prepared to take on the challenges all the way through, which is important, so there's nothing to stop you doing this as a hobby if you keep at it. Although I don't think any circus artists will be too worried about the competition.'

1 In the first paragraph, the writer feels

    A anxious to entertain the people watching.
    B concerned about what was ahead of him.
    C annoyed with the people running the training.
    D unwilling to risk being injured.

2 What does 'this' refer to in line 15?

    A success in the circus
    B having endless enthusiasm
    C achieving a lack of fear
    D acquiring fire-eating skills

3 What does the writer say about fire-eating?

    A He thought it would be foolish of him to do it.
    B He couldn't understand Bryan's instructions.
    C He knew it would leave a bad taste in his mouth.
    D He didn't manage to keep the fire burning.

4 In the third paragraph, what does the writer tell us about the bungee trapeze?

    A He used it in a completely unexpected way.
    B He saw it as an opportunity to show his courage.
    C He was lucky to complete the trick safely.
    D He discovered he really enjoyed this activity.

5 What do we learn about Moira?

    A Her methods were rather complicated.
    B She seemed to move with little effort.
    C Her upbringing was slightly unusual.
    D She was quite impatient to get started.

6 What is the writer's opinion of his performance in the fifth paragraph?

    A He did the first trick so well that he tried a different one.
    B He should have chosen to do some more impressive tricks.
    C He found it hard to get into position for the first trick.
    D He thought the first trick he performed was too easy.

7 What does 'bring the house down' mean in line 57?

    A run about in a crazy manner
    B all ask for their money back
    C become furious
    D clap wildly

8 In the last paragraph, Nick suggests that the writer

    A could make a career as a circus artist if he wanted to.
    B should not be afraid to take part in circus competitions.
    C has the right attitude towards performing circus tricks.
    D should not be put off by the hard work involved in the circus.

Reading Part 2

You are going to read an article about a teenage inventor. Seven sentences have been removed from the article. Choose from the sentences **A – H** the one which fits each gap (**9 – 15**). There is one extra sentence which you do not need to use.
Mark your answers **on the separate answer sheet**.

Teenage inventor

Not every teenager carries a business card reading 'Inventor' and is friends with their town's mayor. Then again, Gina Gallant was never an average teenager. She was travelling in the car with her family past an enormous rubbish tip when the idea came to her that perhaps the waste materials could be used to make new roads.

Upon returning home, Gina began researching environmentally friendly road-building materials. **9** She had a feeling, however, that plastic, which takes up one third of all space in rubbish tips worldwide, was just the right ingredient.

10 It was, after all, just one of a handful of projects that she had already tackled over the years. Inspired by her father, a chemical technologist, and encouraged by her own natural curiosity, Gina started inventing at a very young age. When she was ten, she developed a substance that remains solid in a liquid base for ten minutes, because she wanted to prevent crackers from going soft when she dipped them in her soup. Gina called her secret ingredient 'Substance G'.

Her second invention was a bicycle helmet that lights up at the front and at the back when a child wears it correctly. Gina was inspired to invent this when her little brother had an accident on his bike. He could have been seriously hurt, but wasn't because his bicycle helmet was properly secured. **11** She spent 300 hours working out how to make a standard helmet safe for all kids. According to the Bicycle Helmet Institute, she succeeded. She attached small lights to a standard helmet. The lights only light up when the helmet is on the child's head in the safest position, leading to a somewhat space-age style which kids love.

But Gina's introduction to the world of business would take place by converting used plastic milk containers into road surfaces. Gina says, 'People looked at me as if I was crazy at first.' **12** This came when the petroleum company where her father worked decided to help her. With them, she learned how to mix plastic with sand and other road-building materials and managed to create the perfect mixture.

13 To do this she suggested the idea of testing the mixture to the mayor of her town. 'I thought it sounded like a good idea because we're always faced with the challenge of cutting down our waste,' he said. The mayor allowed her to use a 500-metre stretch of road outside the town as a test site.

Soon, a number of businesses were interested in becoming involved. One company agreed to provide recycled plastic; another tested the quality of the road surface; and a local company built the actual test road. They told her they would help her with the physical work but she had to lead the team through the process. **14**

With a great deal of attention from the media, the determined teenager completed her project. She gave a lot of interviews to the press. **15** She said her previous inventions had received media attention in the past so people already knew about her, and when everyone began to take notice of her new project, she had already devoted thousands of hours to it.

A	Inventing a road-building material was an ambitious new challenge for her, but Gina was not easily put off.	**E**	She was now eager to try out her invention in a real-world situation.
B	Although when they heard of her desire to reuse plastic, approximately 70 of them brought their waste plastic to her home.	**F**	The fact that success didn't just happen overnight was something she always stressed in these.
C	Gina happily agreed to take on this responsibility and impressed everybody.	**G**	She carried on with her idea, however, until she finally had a breakthrough.
D	It turned out that glass and rubber had been used before, but with poor results.	**H**	As a result of this incident, Gina naturally felt very motivated.

Reading Part 3

Questions 16 – 30

You are going to read an article in which four teenagers talk about their free-time activities and hobbies. For questions **16 – 30**, choose from options (**A – D**). The options may be chosen more than once.
Mark your answers **on the separate answer sheet**.

Which person

has to pay for what they need for their hobby themselves?

16 ☐

is grateful for the encouragement they have received from others?

17 ☐

stresses the importance of the location for their hobby?

18 ☐

says their hobby has been useful for their studies?

19 ☐

has found the weather to be a problem at times?

20 ☐

wishes a particular person approved of their chosen activity?

21 ☐

is rarely satisfied with what they have done?

22 ☐

says that their friends don't always cooperate?

23 ☐

sometimes has access to equipment that is not theirs?

24 ☐

finds the name of their hobby is sometimes misunderstood?

25 ☐

has inspired other people to take up their hobby?

26 ☐

considers that they are improving their skills?

27 ☐

says that their hobby is less expensive than is sometimes thought?

28 ☐

feels a little annoyed by the reaction to them in certain places?

29 ☐

makes sure they are always ready to do their activity?

30 ☐

Free-time activities

A Maria

What I really love doing in my free time is painting. Sometimes when I tell people that, they ask me if I can come and decorate their houses for them, which is quite funny really. My grandfather used to paint landscapes and I'd go out for the day with him. He gave me a lovely little painting set with all the stuff I needed and I've never got rid of it. I prefer painting outdoors when I can, but sometimes my fingers get too cold to hold the brush properly, so I have to take a photograph and finish the picture at home. I also do portraits, but that's not exactly easy to do well. No one of my age that I know can be bothered to sit still for more than a few minutes! Some art galleries are really cool, and give me the chance to see what real artists have done. Sometimes I'll stay in front of the same painting for hours on end. I do stand out a bit though; sometimes I think people are staring at me just because of the age I am – which gets on my nerves sometimes!

B Luke

You'll never catch me without my camera, whatever the weather, just in case. I take loads of pictures, but only one in every 20 or so actually makes it onto my computer, and out of those only a few will be good enough to keep. I got a camera for my tenth birthday. I lost that one ages ago, but it would be out of date by now anyway – the one I have now is so much better, but half the price. A good eye makes all the difference and I'm developing that, and of course I do have some natural ability – or at least that's what I've been told, and that sort of positive feedback is always welcome. My friends often ask me for copies of what I've taken, so that must mean something, too. And my Art teacher asked me to take pictures at our end-of-term party. Maybe I'll earn my living from my hobby one day!

C Sarah

Some people think that staring at stars is a bit of a weird thing to do, but some of my friends are into astronomy, too. It probably wouldn't have crossed my mind to get involved in something like that unless my Physics teacher had set up a club at school. It's really great to be able to study a subject in depth like that. People don't always understand that you don't need a great deal of cash to get involved in astronomy. Having your own telescope isn't a requirement; the one at school is at our disposal when there's something particularly interesting happening, and we have a special observation evening. We take the telescope out into a field nearby and watch from there. You can also see a lot just by looking out of your window, or standing in the garden – but you do need a warm coat! I live in the middle of nowhere, so the sky is quite dark at night and I can actually see stars and planets clearly. That really makes a difference.

D Eric

My mum thought I was mad when I started flying model aeroplanes, but when she saw how much I liked it, she realised it wasn't just a phase and stopped teasing me about it, even though she still doesn't really see the point of it. It would be nice if she did. I enjoy myself whether it's freezing cold or the sun is shining, and there are lots of good places near my home where I can go. I'm always getting better and better models, which cost me a lot, so I have a Saturday job, too. My friends like to come along once in a while so they can have a go, and some of them are even saving up for their own models now. Making the models and flying them has helped me understand some of my school Physics, which is encouraging, and I'm glad I have a good reason to get outside and not just stay indoors watching TV, which is pretty much all some of my friends do.

Paper 2 (1 hour and 20 minutes)
Writing Part 1

You **must** answer this question. Write your answer in **120 – 150** words in an appropriate style.

1   You have received a letter from the editor of an English film magazine, Mr James Green. Read Mr Green's letter and the notes you have made. Then write a letter to Mr Green, using **all** your notes.

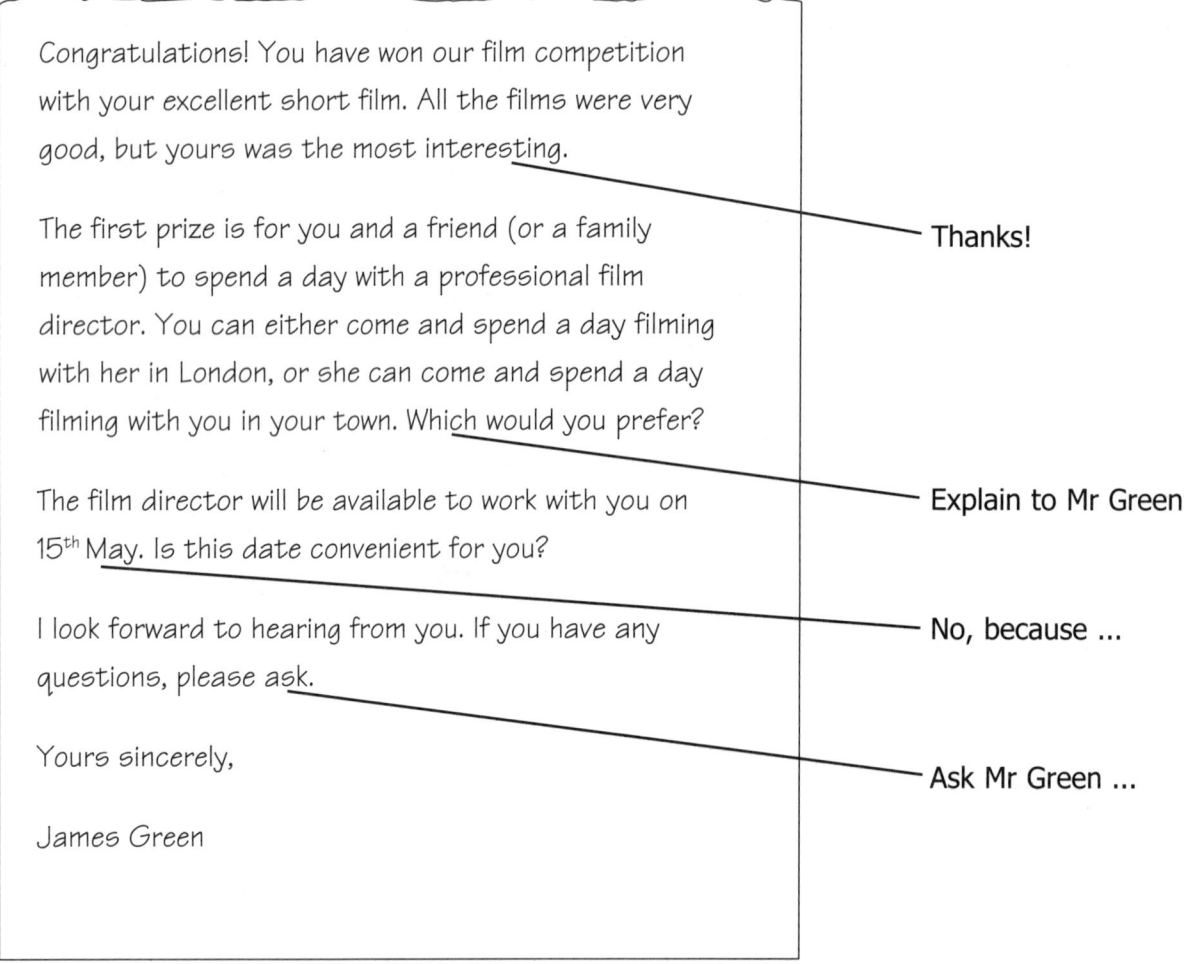

Congratulations! You have won our film competition with your excellent short film. All the films were very good, but yours was the most interesting.
— Thanks!

The first prize is for you and a friend (or a family member) to spend a day with a professional film director. You can either come and spend a day filming with her in London, or she can come and spend a day filming with you in your town. Which would you prefer?
— Explain to Mr Green

The film director will be available to work with you on 15th May. Is this date convenient for you?
— No, because ...

I look forward to hearing from you. If you have any questions, please ask.
— Ask Mr Green ...

Yours sincerely,

James Green

Write your **letter**. You must use grammatically correct sentences with accurate spelling and punctuation in a style appropriate for the situation.

Writing Part 2

Questions 2 – 5

Write an answer to **one** of the questions **2 – 5** in this part. Write your answer in **120 – 180** words in an appropriate style.

---

2   You have decided to enter a short-story competition in an international magazine.

Your story must **begin** with this sentence.

Although she felt quite nervous, Laura smiled as she walked into the room.

Write your **story**.

3   Your English teacher would like to set up a cycling club at your school. She has asked you to write a report for homework giving your suggestions about where people could cycle, what sort of activities the club could organise, and how it could attract as many members as possible.

Write your **report**.

4   You see this announcement on an English-language website.

Articles wanted!

Special Places

Tell us about a place that is special to you.
What do you do there?
Why is it important in your life?

The best articles will be published on our website next month.

Write your **article**.

5   Set text questions. (Please note there are no set text questions included in this practice test.)

Paper 3 (45 minutes)

Use of English Part 1

Questions 1 – 12

For questions **1 – 12**, read the text below and decide which answer (**A**, **B**, **C** or **D**) best fits each gap. There is an example at the beginning (**0**).
Mark your answers **on the separate answer sheet**.

Example:

0   **A**   elderly   **B**   ancient   **C**   past   **D**   antique

0	A	B	C	D
	☐	■	☐	☐

Stonehenge

Stonehenge is probably the most important **(0)** .... monument in the whole of Britain. It is made of enormous stones and stands on flat ground in southern England. For hundreds of years, people have come to **(1)** .... at its mysterious beauty. What visitors to Stonehenge see today is the final **(2)** .... of the work completed about 3,500 years ago, but experts believe its history **(3)** .... back to around 5,000 years ago. The first Stonehenge was basically a large pile of earth surrounded by round holes and was probably built around 3100 BC. **(4)** .... after this, Stonehenge was abandoned for over 1,000 years.

The second and most dramatic phase of the building of Stonehenge started around 2150 BC. In an astonishing journey **(5)** .... nearly 380 km, 82 large stones were transported to the site from mountains in the south-west of Britain. It is **(6)** .... these stones, some of which weigh four tonnes, were **(7)** .... dragged from the mountains to the **(8)** .... From there they were **(9)** .... by sea and up two rivers, then dragged over **(10)** .... again to their destination. **(11)** .... at the site, the stones were set up in the centre to form the nearly **(12)** .... double circle that is still there today.

1	**A**	gaze	**B**	watch	**C**	glance	**D**	observe
2	**A**	period	**B**	step	**C**	point	**D**	stage
3	**A**	turns	**B**	dates	**C**	looks	**D**	gets
4	**A**	Rapidly	**B**	Promptly	**C**	Shortly	**D**	Quickly
5	**A**	covering	**B**	going	**C**	travelling	**D**	wandering
6	**A**	hoped	**B**	thought	**C**	wondered	**D**	expected
7	**A**	likely	**B**	somehow	**C**	hardly	**D**	anyway
8	**A**	coast	**B**	bank	**C**	edge	**D**	border
9	**A**	passed	**B**	lifted	**C**	carried	**D**	loaded
10	**A**	country	**B**	territory	**C**	earth	**D**	land
11	**A**	After	**B**	Once	**C**	Since	**D**	Yet
12	**A**	overall	**B**	total	**C**	complete	**D**	full

Use of English Part 2

Questions 13 – 24

For questions **13 – 24**, read the text below and think of the word which best fits each gap. Use only one word in each gap. There is an example at the beginning (**0**).
Write your answers **IN CAPITAL LETTERS on the separate answer sheet**.

Example: | **0** | T | H | E | | | | | | | | | | | | | | | |

Whales Learn Songs

Humpback whales are amongst **(0)** .... largest species of whales. **(13)** .... has been known for many years that male humpback whales sing – but did you know that one group of whales can learn the songs sung by a different group? **(14)** .... than simply consisting of a series of random noises, the songs contain themes that keep repeating and developing. Also, the whales produce a new song **(15)** .... year. While scientists have been aware for **(16)** .... time that the entire population of male whales in a group sing the 'song of the year', they have now discovered, **(17)** .... many people's surprise, that this song is also 'downloaded' by whales in other areas of the world!

Biologists recorded songs from different whale populations for 12 years. **(18)** .... they observed was amazing. Most of the songs originally came from a humpback group living near Australia. The same songs then moved from group to group, until they **(19)** .... being sung by whales living about 6,500 km **(20)** .... The scientists are not sure **(21)** .... the songs are passed **(22)** .... by male humpbacks who move from one group to **(23)** .... or shared by the different groups when they meet. The discovery confirms that **(24)** .... humans, whales exchange their culture with each other.

Use of English Part 3

Questions 25 – 34

For questions **25 – 34**, read the text below. Use the word given in capitals at the end of some of the lines to form a word that fits in the gap in the **same line**. There is an example at the beginning (**0**). Write your answers **IN CAPITAL LETTERS on the separate answer sheet**.

Example:

0	R	E	A	L	I	T	Y												

How to Become a Fashion Designer

If you're thinking of becoming a teenage fashion designer, here are some tips to help you turn your dreams into (**0**) .... It can all seem pretty **REAL**
scary! No matter how (**25**) .... it may seem now though, there are **POSSIBLE**
things you can do.

You need to start thinking like all the (**26**) .... designers out there. First **SUCCEED**
of all, educate yourself. Study fashion magazines. Are there any
(**27**) .... between your style and the current trends? What makes you **SIMILAR**
unique? Questions like these will get you thinking (**28**) .... about what **CARE**
your own personal style is.

It may seem (**29**) .... but really take time to learn about colours. **ELEMENT**
From there, move on to cloth. It takes time and (**30**) .... to learn how **PATIENT**
different materials feel and how they move, but it's (**31**) .... worthwhile. **DEFINE**

Produce (**32**) .... designs for yourself and wear them when you go to **ORIGIN**
parties, the movies, wherever! Show everyone how (**33**) .... you are, **CREATE**
and if your friends and family like the look, make clothes for them. Finally,
if you want (**34**) .... about courses you could do in the future, discuss **RECOMMEND**
your plans with your Art teacher. Believe in yourself – you can make it!

Use of English Part 4

Questions 35 – 42

For questions **35 – 42**, complete the second sentence so that it has a similar meaning to the first sentence, using the word given. **Do not change the word given.** You must use between **two** and **five** words, including the word given. Here is an example (**0**).

Example:

0   Don't worry, the teacher will show us exactly what to do.

   SHOWN

   Don't worry, ... what to do by the teacher.

The gap can be filled by the words 'we will be shown exactly' so you write:

Example: | **0** | WE WILL BE SHOWN EXACTLY

Write **only** the missing words **IN CAPITAL LETTERS on the separate answer sheet**.

---

35   Djamel plays the trumpet much better than anyone else in his school.

   FAR

   Djamel is by .... in his school.

36   Perhaps Tomas forgot to take his phone with him when he went out this morning.

   MAY

   Tomas .... to take his phone with him when he went out this morning.

37   Whenever I smell that perfume, I remember my Aunt Amy.

   REMINDS

   Whenever I smell that perfume, ... my Aunt Amy.

38   Because Jo performed so brilliantly, our school won the drama competition.

   RESULT

   As .... brilliant performance, our school won the drama competition.

39 Luisa was very excited because she had succeeded in buying some tickets to see her favourite band.

ABLE

Luisa was very excited because she had .... some tickets to see her favourite band.

40 It's a pity we aren't sitting a bit further away from the cinema screen.

WISH

I .... sitting so close to the cinema screen.

41 I didn't expect that topic to be mentioned during our class discussion.

COME

I didn't think that topic .... during our class discussion.

42 Please don't whistle that annoying tune!

MIND

Would .... that annoying tune?

Paper 4 (approximately 40 minutes)

Listening Part 1

Questions 1 – 8

You will hear people talking in eight different situations. For questions **1 – 8**, choose the best answer (**A, B** or **C**).

1   You hear two friends talking about a computer game called *Racquet King*.
    What do they agree about?

   A   how fast it is

   B   how good it is

   C   how realistic it is

2   You walk past a classroom and hear the teacher talking to the students.
    What is the subject of the lesson?

   A   Maths

   B   Biology

   C   Geography

3   You hear a brother and his sister talking about a holiday.
    Where are they going to go?

   A   a city

   B   the beach

   C   the mountains

4   You hear a boy talking to a friend about a school play he has acted in.
    How does he feel now?

   A   relieved

   B   annoyed

   C   disappointed

5   You hear a music teacher talking to a school orchestra.
    Why is he talking to them?

    A   to tell them off

    B   to introduce himself

    C   to give them some news

6   You hear two friends talking about a film they have both seen.
    What does the girl think about it?

    A   It has some very good actors in it.

    B   It is funnier than she had expected.

    C   It isn't as good as other films of that type.

7   You hear part of a radio programme.
    What is the woman talking about?

    A   a local sports event

    B   a new leisure centre

    C   a new form of exercise

8   You hear a girl asking about some jeans in a shop.
    Who are the jeans for?

    A   her mother

    B   her brother

    C   herself

Listening Part 2

Questions 9 – 18

You will hear a girl called Jodie talking about a class visit to a city farm. For questions **9 – 18**, complete the sentences.

Class Trip to Bluebells City Farm

Jodie and her class went by [_____ **9**] to Bluebells City Farm.

Jodie noticed the [_____ **10**] when they arrived at the farm.

Jodie's teacher said she used to know kids who didn't know where

[_____ **11**] grew.

Jodie didn't want to touch the [_____ **12**] when she went into the field.

At Bluebells City Farm, [_____ **13**] courses are available.

Jodie thinks she will take her [_____ **14**] to be repaired at the farm.

Jodie had a [_____ **15**] at the café at lunchtime.

Some of Jodie's classmates didn't like the [_____ **16**] on the farm.

It cost Jodie's class nothing to get into the farm, but they paid

[_____ **17**] pounds towards the cost of feeding the animals.

Now Jodie and her classmates have to write a [_____ **18**] for the teacher about their visit to the farm.

Listening Part 3

Questions 19 – 23

You will hear five different people talking about things they always carry with them. For questions **19 – 23**, choose from the list (**A – F**) what each speaker says about why they always carry these things with them. Use the letters only once. There is one extra letter which you do not need to use.

A	It is something I need to use every day.	Speaker 1 **19** ☐
B	It reminds me of someone I care about.	Speaker 2 **20** ☐
C	It is something I use when I'm bored.	Speaker 3 **21** ☐
D	It makes me feel safe.	Speaker 4 **22** ☐
E	It is part of a joke I share with my friends.	Speaker 5 **23** ☐
F	It is something I find beautiful.	

Listening Part 4

Questions 24 – 30

You will hear an interview with a boy called Leon Honnor about some party nights for 12 to 15 year olds.
For questions **24 – 30**, choose the best answer (**A**, **B** or **C**).

24 Why did Leon and his friend think of having a party night?

    A   They only wanted to mix with people they knew.

    B   They wanted to enjoy themselves in a secure place.

    C   They couldn't afford to go anywhere in their town.

25 What does Leon say about setting up the party night?

    A   The manager of the building wouldn't help.

    B   Somebody else had already had the same idea.

    C   The owners of the building organised it all.

26 What is the venue like?

    A   The top-floor lights are special.

    B   People can cool down outdoors.

    C   There are seats by the dance floor.

27 When asked about the food, Leon says that

    A   it is better than people might expect.

    B   they serve fast food or fresh food.

    C   all the food costs the same amount.

28 How does Leon feel about the rules at the party nights?

    A   He wishes he could take a bag in.

    B   He thinks the chewing gum ban is too strict.

    C   He would prefer it if rules were unnecessary.

29 How can people pay less for a ticket?

    A by showing a previous ticket

    B by paying a membership fee

    C by buying tickets in advance

30 Leon says one reason why people should go to the next party night is

    A to see a famous band.

    B to celebrate his birthday.

    C to get to know new people.

Paper 5

About the Speaking test

Part 1 (3 minutes)

In this part of the test, the examiner asks you and your partner some questions about yourselves. You may be asked questions about 'your family', 'your school', 'your free time', etc.

Part 2 (one-minute response from each candidate, plus a 20-second response from the second candidate)

In this part of the test, the examiner gives you two photos to talk about for one minute. The examiner then asks your partner a question about the photos and your partner responds briefly.

The examiner then gives two different photos to your partner to talk about. Afterwards, the examiner will ask you a question about your partner's photos and you respond briefly.

Part 3 (3 minutes)

In this part of the test, the examiner asks you and your partner to talk together. You may be asked to find a solution to a problem, or to decide something. For example, you may be asked to discuss the best place to visit on a school trip. The examiner gives you a picture with some ideas you can use, but does not join in the conversation.

Part 4 (4 minutes)

In this part of the test, the examiner asks you and your partner in turn some further questions in relation to what you have discussed in Part 3. You can also comment on your partner's answers.

Test 2

Paper 1 (1 hour)

Reading Part 1

Questions 1 – 8

You are going to read an article about a visit to a famous rock in Australia, called Uluru. For questions
1 – 8, choose the answer (**A**, **B**, **C** or **D**) which you think fits best according to the text.
Mark your answers **on the separate answer sheet**.

My Visit to Uluru Rock

I've lived in Australia all my life but have never travelled inland to see one of my country's most famous sights – the Uluru rock. So I jumped at the chance to travel there with a bunch of students and teachers from my school during our holidays. I was bothered about travelling with one or two of my classmates because we'd never been particularly friendly and I wasn't sure how I'd feel about going away without my parents for the first time either. I needn't have worried though because it was truly worthwhile. I thought our teachers were pretty cool about the whole thing, though they still had their list of dos and don'ts!

We flew to the national park in which the rock is located. I'd never been on a plane before so that was almost as exciting as seeing the rock itself. We arrived at the airport early which meant hanging around for a while. Some of the students complained because they found the whole airport thing pretty dull, but I could hardly take my eyes off the fascinating destinations board. I passed the time day-dreaming and eventually, we made our way to the gate. I was almost disappointed when the journey passed with barely a bump!

Once we'd touched down, we were transported to our accommodation: Uhuru Campground. It was from the bus that we caught our first glimpse of Uluru and I couldn't tear my eyes away from this huge rock sticking out of the bush-covered land spreading out around it. It's a special site for the Aboriginal people who've lived in the area for thousands of years, and I could see the reason for so much outside interest. What an impact it had – everyone went quiet for a few moments before starting to chatter excitedly.

At the campground we cooled off in the pool before dinner. Then it was time for the moment we'd all been looking forward to – sunset over the rock. I was convinced there was

no way it would live up to expectations, but it was everything I could have hoped for and more. I'd imagined it being a peaceful event, but we had to go to a special viewing area with lots of other people. I blocked out their light-hearted gossip though. The sunset was unlike anything I'd seen before: the rock glowed orange while the land around it went dark.

Our teacher filled us in on a few facts about the rock. Uluru doesn't mean 'waterhole' as is often reported, but it simply refers to the rock and the waterhole on top. The rock is a sacred place for the Aboriginal people, so they ask people not to climb the rock because of its significance to their culture and the ceremonies they perform there. I think it's vital to respect people's cultures, so I didn't mind when our teacher told us we'd be walking around it instead of climbing it.

The walk around the base of Uluru was awe-inspiring. The rock is full of holes and very bare, with hardly a plant growing from it. I didn't mind the long walk because our guide was really interesting. He told us all about the rock and its history and pointed out areas that we couldn't go to because they're private and meaningful places for the Aboriginal people who live there. This made the whole experience so much more special and I got to understand the real importance of the rock to Australia and its people.

Tired and dusty we returned to the camp and I scribbled everything down in my journal. Then there was time to chat with the other guests. There were people from all over the world and they had amazing tales about their adventures while travelling through Australia and the people they had met along the way. My schoolmates and teachers sat around the campfire with them and I thought about everything I'd seen and learned. I felt proud to be Australian and I'll never forget my trip to Uluru.

43

63

1   How did the writer feel when he heard about the trip to the interior of Australia?

   A   concerned that he wouldn't get on with his schoolmates
   B   nervous about travelling with people he didn't know
   C   anxious that his teachers would be too strict
   D   worried that he would miss his family

2   What does the writer say about his experience of flying?

   A   He hadn't expected to enjoy the atmosphere of the airport so much.
   B   He couldn't understand why other students didn't share his feelings.
   C   He thought the wait for the flight was too long.
   D   He hoped that the flight would be more eventful than it was.

3   What does the writer say about his first sight of Uluru?

   A   He appreciated why it attracts so much attention.
   B   He was impressed by the landscape surrounding it.
   C   He recognised why Aboriginal people settled there.
   D   He wondered why it made his travel companions go silent.

4   When talking about viewing the sunset over the rock, the writer suggests that

   A   the experience was a quiet and thoughtful one for the viewers.
   B   the atmosphere was spoiled by the presence of so many people.
   C   the evening light on the rock was a unique sight.
   D   the event was unexpectedly disappointing.

5   What does 'sacred' mean in line 43?

   A   spiritual
   B   famous
   C   safe
   D   useful

6   In the fifth paragraph, what opinion does the writer express?

   A   People are careless about getting facts right.
   B   People should try to take others' beliefs into account.
   C   People often ignore the wishes of other people.
   D   People are right to inform others of their traditions.

7   In the sixth paragraph, what is the writer doing?

   A   explaining the guide's feelings for the rock
   B   describing the lifestyle of local people
   C   expressing his knowledge of history
   D   giving readers information about the rock

8   Who does 'them' refer to in line 63?

   A   other Australians
   B   the writer's teachers
   C   foreign tourists
   D   the writer's school friends

Reading Part 2

Questions 9 – 15

You are going to read a review of a book about BMXing, a style of bicycle racing. Seven sentences have been removed from the review. Choose from the sentences **A – H** the one which fits each gap (**9 – 15**). There is one extra sentence which you do not need to use.
Mark your answers **on the separate answer sheet**.

Book review - *I love my BMX*

I've just read *I love my BMX* by Joanna Kennedy. It's a great read – not just for people who do the sport itself, but for anyone who has a passion for any kind of sport or activity. **9** [   ] That's because she teaches you in the book that with a bit of determination and motivation you can achieve anything.

If you don't know anything about BMXing, this book is a great place to start. I learned that BMX stands for 'bicycle motocross', which is a style of extreme bicycle racing and it's also the name for the kind of bike used too. **10** [   ] This is really exciting to watch and though I've never tried it, I think it would give you even more of a buzz taking part.

The book starts with a brief history of BMXing and tells us how the first BMX bikes were built to replicate motorcycles – without an engine of course. **11** [   ] BMXing became widespread after a film was launched in the cinema called *On Any Sunday* and now it's an Olympic sport! I really want to watch the film now I've read this book, though it's quite old.

Joanna started BMXing when she was young and then got her brothers into it too. From a really young age she was fixing her bike herself and she admits that she spent every minute outside practising riding in the woods near where she lived. She talks a bit about what it's like being female in a male-dominated sport, but it doesn't seem to be any kind of a problem for her. **12** [   ] She's still only a teenager but she goes into schools and promotes the sport and wants to get more girls involved.

Joanna's raced in loads of competitions and has won lots of medals and trophies. She describes some of her tricks and how she perfected them, which is amazing. **13** [   ] I think that's a really important attitude to have towards anything you're doing – whether it's your Maths homework or learning to ski. Well, they say practice makes perfect, don't they?

I think the way the story is written is great because it's a real page-turner. It's funny in some places and even a little bit sad in others. **14** [   ] She talks about it almost like it's human and she even has a special name for it. That's quite a funny story so I won't ruin it. You'll have to read the book to find out. Now she's made her name in the BMX world, Joanna's lent the bike to a museum so people can go and see it.

I'm really interested to see how Joanna does in her next international competition. It's a really big event and I've been following her progress since I read the book. **15** [   ] It's going to be about her experiences competing all over the world.

A	I only picked up the book in the first place because I found it lying around at home.	**E**	Racers compete against each other on tracks, usually made of earth, and perform tricks as they ride, such as difficult turns and jumps.
B	Like when she had to stop riding her first and favourite bike because she grew too tall for it.	**F**	The book doesn't really explain why people started doing this but I guess it was because it was a cheaper option for kids.
C	I suppose there's no reason why it should be.	**G**	I've heard she's going to write another one too so I can't wait for that.
D	She writes from the heart and I think it's a really inspirational read.	**H**	She just wouldn't stop until she got them right.

Reading Part 3

Questions 16 – 30

You are going to read about four people describing their holiday experiences. For questions **16 – 30**, choose from options (**A – D**). The options may be chosen more than once.
Mark your answers **on the separate answer sheet**.

Which person

is happy not to go to other countries again?

16 ☐

doesn't want to cause problems for others on holiday?

17 ☐

enjoys practising a hobby on a particular type of holiday?

18 ☐

only takes holidays in their own country?

19 ☐

thinks it would be interesting to travel more widely?

20 ☐

gets frustrated with a certain type of holiday?

21 ☐

developed a practical skill on holiday?

22 ☐

turned an unfavourable situation into something more fun?

23 ☐

discovered a fun game with a family member?

24 ☐

takes part in a traditional activity on holiday?

25 ☐

says they spend too much time with adults on holiday?

26 ☐

divides their time between different groups of people during their holidays?

27 ☐

doesn't mind a particular inconvenience on holiday?

28 ☐

feels lucky to have experienced things other people haven't?

29 ☐

enjoys spending time with people they don't often see?

30 ☐

Holidays

A Joanna

I've never been to another country on holiday – it's not really what people do where I come from. Lots of people have a small house in the countryside and we go away with all the family for a month every summer. I go with my parents, aunt, uncle and cousins. For me it's the best part of the year because we don't get together very often. I don't have any brothers or sisters, so getting to hang out with my cousins is great – we're all into the same kind of things. There's a lake near our cottage and when it's hot we go and splash around and the adults sit and chat or go for walks. One of the things people do in my country is collect wild mushrooms. You have to know what you're looking for, but I love going along. In the evenings we sing and make campfires and eat together. It's so relaxing; I feel like I'm a thousand kilometres from school. It would be nice to see another country, too, I guess – maybe when I've got some money of my own.

B Ken

I'm fortunate in that I've been to lots of places with my family – not everyone has the opportunity to do that. I'm an only child, so I guess I'm a bit spoiled that way. I love visiting cities and getting to know the history of places. I'm really into photography, so I love taking pictures of old buildings and monuments. Beach holidays are probably my least favourite kind of holiday. There's not much for me to do because my parents like to sit around and sunbathe and I find it a bit boring. I'd rather spend more time with people my own age. I try to make friends and go snorkelling and swimming, but it's not great on your own. I've asked if my friend can come away with us this summer so I hope he can; it'll be nice being with another young person. My favourite holiday was when we stayed at my uncle's house in the mountains. It was so much fun, even though we stayed in our own country.

C Mario

I love messing about by the beach on holiday. My friend's parents have an apartment on the coast and go there every holiday. I go with them in summer for a week or so when my parents are working. Sometimes I go abroad with my parents later. We have loads of fun swimming or going for rides on our bikes. My friend's parents are always looking out for us, so we don't go too far away – I wouldn't want them to worry. I never want to go back to the city. I once spent the whole of my school holidays there and it was so dull because everyone else had gone away. I didn't know what to do with myself at first, but then I thought about all the things I'd never done in the city and I did little trips every day. Sometimes I went with my grandma and we visited museums or went for lunch in a café, or looked around the shops. It was a different kind of holiday!

D Bella

My sister's a lot older than me and when she got married she bought a caravan with her husband so they could travel about together. They've got two kids and I've been on a few weekends away with them and my mum comes, too. It's great fun, though it's a bit of a squeeze in the caravan. But I don't mind sharing with my nieces. We cook together on a campfire and that's the bit I love best. I can make a few things now like baked potatoes and pasta. We sit around in the evening playing games and singing songs. My favourite time was when we stayed by the beach – it was really stony and my brother-in-law taught me how to bounce stones off the water. We had a great time competing against each other! I've only been to another country once, but I was glad to come back home – I couldn't understand a word and it was so frustrating! Maybe I'll try again one day, but I'm not bothered.

Paper 2 (1 hour and 20 minutes)
Writing Part 1

You **must** answer this question. Write your answer in **120 – 150** words in an appropriate style.

1   You have received an email from your English-speaking friend, Chris. Read Chris's email and the notes you have made. Then write an email to Chris, using **all** your notes.

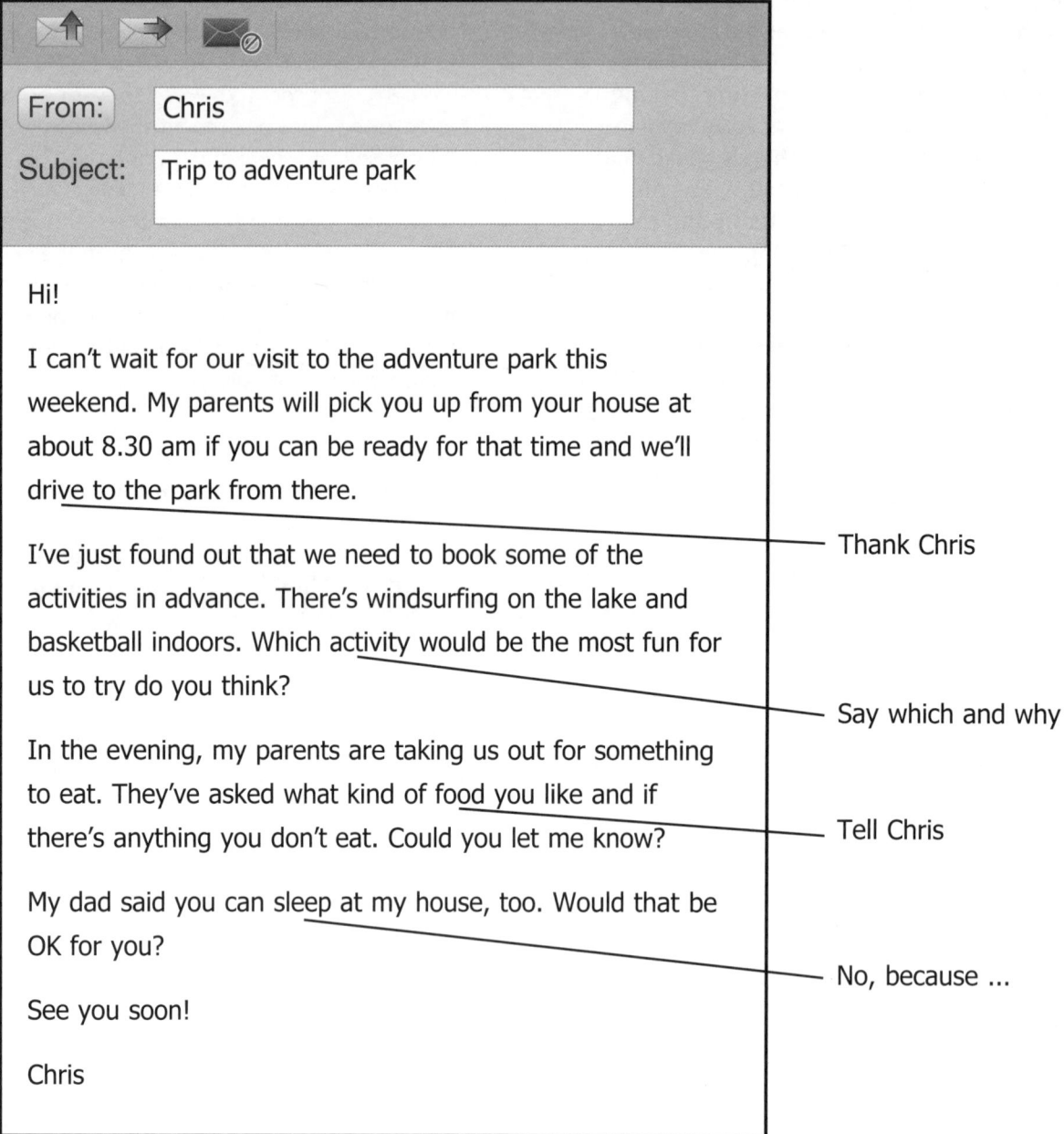

From: Chris

Subject: Trip to adventure park

Hi!

I can't wait for our visit to the adventure park this weekend. My parents will pick you up from your house at about 8.30 am if you can be ready for that time and we'll drive to the park from there. ———— Thank Chris

I've just found out that we need to book some of the activities in advance. There's windsurfing on the lake and basketball indoors. Which activity would be the most fun for us to try do you think? ———— Say which and why

In the evening, my parents are taking us out for something to eat. They've asked what kind of food you like and if there's anything you don't eat. Could you let me know? ———— Tell Chris

My dad said you can sleep at my house, too. Would that be OK for you? ———— No, because ...

See you soon!

Chris

Write your **email**. You must use grammatically correct sentences with accurate spelling and punctuation in a style appropriate for the situation.

Writing Part 2

Questions 2 – 5

Write an answer to **one** of the questions **2 – 5** in this part. Write your answer in **120 – 180** words in an appropriate style.

---

2 Here is part of a letter you have received from Lori, your English-speaking friend.

I've just celebrated my country's national day. It was fun!
My family and friends ate special food, sang songs and wore new clothes. What do you celebrate in your country? How do you celebrate? Do you think traditions are important?

From

Lori

Write your **letter**.

3 You have had a discussion in your English class about learning from older people. Your teacher has asked you to write an essay giving your opinions on the following question.

What do you think young people can learn from older generations in your country?

Write your **essay**.

4 You have recently seen this notice in an English-language magazine.

We need your reviews!

Have you used a good website recently? If so, could you write us a review of the website? Tell us what you liked about it and why you would recommend it to other people.

We'll publish the best reviews in our magazine next month.

Write your **review**.

5 Set text questions. (Please note there are no set text questions included in this practice test.)

Paper 3 (45 minutes)
Use of English Part 1

Questions 1 – 12

For questions **1 – 12**, read the text below and decide which answer (**A**, **B**, **C** or **D**) best fits each gap. There is an example at the beginning (**0**).
Mark your answers **on the separate answer sheet**.

Example:

0 **A** noticing **B** watching **C** seeing **D** staring

0	A B C D
	☐ ☐ ☐ ■

Teenagers need more sleep!

It's 8 am on a school-day morning and Paolo is **(0)** .... at his teacher as she **(1)** .... about what they're going to do in class that day. Science is one of Paolo's favourite subjects, but he just can't seem to **(2)** .... awake!

Recent **(3)** .... has shown that teenagers can't be **(4)** .... to make the most of their classes early in the morning. Their eyes may be open but their brains are still asleep, say experts. After a weekend of sitting up late chatting to friends on the internet, or watching films until the early **(5)** .... it's no surprise that the first day of the week is difficult. Having changing **(6)** .... of sleep between week and weekend days mean many teens suffer the **(7)** .... in their first classes of the day. **(8)** .... many school bells continue to ring at 7.30 am

According to the study, teens need at least an hour more sleep than adults in order to function **(9)** .... at school and they don't feel sleepy until later at night. The **(10)** .... ? Schools need to change their timetables and students should take time to relax for **(11)** .... before going to bed. That also means **(12)** .... more late-night texting!

1	**A**	discusses	**B**	talks	**C**	mentions	**D**	informs
2	**A**	stay	**B**	be	**C**	manage	**D**	stop
3	**A**	experience	**B**	examination	**C**	research	**D**	action
4	**A**	thought	**B**	assumed	**C**	predicted	**D**	expected
5	**A**	time	**B**	moments	**C**	hours	**D**	period
6	**A**	structures	**B**	patterns	**C**	arrangements	**D**	styles
7	**A**	problems	**B**	consequences	**C**	events	**D**	causes
8	**A**	Yet	**B**	Thus	**C**	Despite	**D**	Besides
9	**A**	enough	**B**	right	**C**	suitably	**D**	properly
10	**A**	explanation	**B**	reaction	**C**	solution	**D**	issue
11	**A**	longer	**B**	earlier	**C**	sooner	**D**	better
12	**A**	not	**B**	no	**C**	never	**D**	nothing

Use of English Part 2

Questions 13 – 24

For questions **13 – 24**, read the text below and think of the word which best fits each gap. Use only one word in each gap. There is an example at the beginning (**0**).
Write your answers **IN CAPITAL LETTERS on the separate answer sheet**.

Example:

0	A	F	T	E	R												

Spotting the snow leopard

We sit in our wooden hide-away, day **(0)** .... day. A small group of photographers, we're on a mission to photograph a rare and beautiful animal: the snow leopard. We hope to spot her before too **(13)** .... We've already been here **(14)** .... two weeks and are exhausted **(15)** .... keeping our watchful eye on the rocky slopes of the mountains. It's cold up here, but the views are fantastic.

Seeing one of these stunning creatures in **(16)** .... wild is an unusual event – and one that we are keen to capture. It's **(17)** .... easy sitting bent over the camera for such long periods and **(18)** .... bodies ache from being in the same position for hours **(19)** .... a time. We eat and sleep in shifts **(20)** .... that we don't miss an opportunity to catch the leopard on film forever.

This wonderful animal is known for **(21)** .... difficult to photograph and we know we have to be patient, but we are suffering as we fight tiredness and disappointment.

And then **(22)** .... she is – a female leopard, just metres away from our hiding place! We've finally got our shot and there's a **(23)** .... of celebrating in our den as we prepare to go home at **(24)** ....

Use of English Part 3

Questions 25 – 34

For questions **25 – 34**, read the text below. Use the word given in capitals at the end of some of the lines to form a word that fits in the gap in the **same line**. There is an example at the beginning (**0**). Write your answers **IN CAPITAL LETTERS on the separate answer sheet**.

Example: | **0** | I | M | A | G | I | N | A | T | I | O | N | | | | | | | |

Chocolate tasting for the day

I love chocolate. So, my **(0)** .... ran away with itself when I spotted an advertisement for chocolate tasters online. Yes, I'd read the advert **(25)** .... A large chocolate company based in my town was on the lookout for chocolate tasters.   **IMAGINE**
CORRECT

The advert was so **(26)** .... that I had to re-read the page very **(27)** .... to see if it was really true. The company was offering the chance for six **(28)** .... teenagers to sample their latest flavours of chocolate.   **USUAL**
CARE
LUCK

I filled in an **(29)** .... form online and had to explain why I wanted to do the 'job'. I found the **(30)** .... easy and I wasn't surprised when I got a call saying I'd been asked to join five other tasters for a day at the factory. I can't imagine anyone turning down an **(31)** .... like that!   **EXTEND**
APPLY

INVITE

On the day of the tasting the company staff were really welcoming and we were soon seated **(32)** .... around a large table, ready to begin. There were so many bars to taste I nearly exploded with **(33)** .... All we had to do was write down our thoughts and **(34)** .... about each of the new flavours. We even got to take some chocolate home!   **COMFORT**
EXCITE
FEEL

Use of English Part 4

Questions 35 – 42

For questions **35 – 42**, complete the second sentence so that it has a similar meaning to the first sentence, using the word given. **Do not change the word given.** You must use between **two** and **five** words, including the word given. Here is an example (**0**).

Example:

0 Don't worry, the teacher will show us exactly what to do.

SHOWN

Don't worry, ... what to do by the teacher.

The gap can be filled by the words 'we will be shown exactly' so you write:

Example: | **0** | WE WILL BE SHOWN EXACTLY

Write **only** the missing words **IN CAPITAL LETTERS on the separate answer sheet**.

---

35 I never thought for one minute about inviting Jon to my party – I hardly know him.

CROSSED

It never .... Jon to my party – I hardly know him.

36 Pedro came first in the swimming competition again despite not doing much practice!

SPITE

Pedro came first in the swimming competition again .... that he didn't do much practice!

37 There's no way you saw Penelope in town on Saturday – she was away for the weekend.

HAVE

You .... Penelope in town on Saturday – she was away for the weekend.

38 Sheila doesn't ski well as she doesn't have time to practise.

GOOD

Sheila .... skiing because she doesn't have time to practise.

39 My cycling club mates and I have always had a good relationship.

WELL

I have always .... my cycling club mates.

40 If you text me again at midnight I'm going to be annoyed!

BETTER

You .... me again at midnight or I'll be annoyed.

41 Why don't we go to the skateboard park this weekend?

FANCY

Do .... to the skateboard park this weekend?

42 Hey – our entry fee to the disco includes a free drink!

IS

Hey – a free drink .... the price of the ticket!

Paper 4 (approximately 40 minutes)

Listening Part 1

Questions 1 – 8

You will hear people talking in eight different situations. For questions **1 – 8**, choose the best answer (**A**, **B** or **C**).

1   You hear a teacher talking to his class about a celebration called Earth Day.
    What is the purpose of his talk?

    A   to ask for suggestions

    B   to start a class discussion

    C   to give reasons for something

2   You hear part of a weather forecast.
    What is the speaker doing?

    A   giving a severe-weather warning

    B   suggesting a particular activity

    C   advising people to be careful

3   You hear two friends talking about a world record they have helped to break.
    What do they agree about?

    A   Being on television was unexpected.

    B   Seeing such a large audience was surprising.

    C   Beating their record won't be difficult.

4   You hear a girl telling her friend about a special event she is taking part in.
    What is she most excited about?

    A   wearing a special costume

    B   being part of a large event

    C   dancing with her friends

5 You hear part of a news story about some monkeys that steal visitors' sunglasses in a zoo.
What does the speaker say about the situation?

    A   It's the visitors' fault for getting too near the monkeys.

    B   The zoo has come up with a good solution.

    C   Monkeys are too curious for their own good.

6 You hear a boy talking about being a member of a club.
How does he feel about it?

    A   proud of what he has achieved there

    B   relieved that it is different from school

    C   worried about some of the activities

7 You hear a teacher talking to some students.
What is she talking about?

    A   the best way to learn a language

    B   the benefits of playing computer games

    C   the value of being able to write clearly

8 You hear two friends talking about doing a Chemistry experiment at school.
What does the girl predict?

    A   The experiment probably won't work first time.

    B   The experiment will be difficult to do.

    C   The results of the experiment will be unexpected.

Listening Part 2

Questions 9 – 18

You will hear a TV presenter giving information about a competition called the School Choir of the Year. For questions **9 – 18**, complete the sentences.

School Choir of the Year Competition

Registration forms are to be sent to the organisation's [_____ 9].

Each stage of the competition will close with a [_____ 10].

This year the competition will be held at Redbridge [_____ 11].

The choir name that the speaker liked best was the '[_____ 12] Singers'.

The organisers would especially like to hear some [_____ 13] music this year.

A [_____ 14] is available for use at the venue if the choirs need it.

Choirs should avoid the use of [_____ 15] during their performance.

The speaker suggests a colourful [_____ 16] as an example of what can be worn by participants.

Audience members will have to pay [_____ 17] euros per person to attend the performance.

The winning choir will be invited to perform at the [_____ 18] in Redbridge.

Listening Part 3

Questions 19 – 23

You will hear five different people talking about reading. For questions **19 – 23**, choose from the list (**A – F**) what each speaker says about what they like best about reading. Use the letters only once. There is one extra letter which you do not need to use.

A   I feel like I get to know new kinds of people.

Speaker 1   **19**

B   I like the challenge of reading.

Speaker 2   **20**

C   It's a good way to pass the time when I'm bored.

Speaker 3   **21**

D   It has helped me to develop my personality.

Speaker 4   **22**

E   I learn so much from it.

Speaker 5   **23**

F   I feel like I'm part of the story.

Listening Part 4

Questions 24 – 30

You will hear a girl called Zara talking about being a teenage DJ. For questions **24 – 30**, choose the best answer (**A**, **B** or **C**).

---

24 Zara became interested in being a DJ after

    A   she first heard a certain type of music.

    B   her parents bought her some DJ equipment.

    C   she listened to her parents' music collection.

25 How did Zara feel when she won a teenage DJ competition?

    A   disappointed there were so few people taking part

    B   surprised by the quality of the prize she won

    C   pleased that the audience liked her music

26 What does Zara say about meeting her favourite DJ?

    A   She felt less excited than she expected.

    B   She received unexpected praise.

    C   She was greatly affected by his work.

27 When Zara went to the radio studios she enjoyed

    A   listening to other DJs play.

    B   meeting her musical heroes.

    C   choosing music to play.

28 Zara believes that being a good DJ

    A   is a skill that can be learned.

    B   requires a lot of self-confidence.

    C   gives you a greater understanding of music.

29 What does Zara say about playing music for her friends?

  A It provides her with useful feedback.

  B It is starting to lose its appeal.

  C It helps her to know them better.

30 Zara says that creating a party atmosphere

  A depends on the mood of the crowd.

  B requires her to play music she isn't keen on.

  C places demands on her creativity.

Paper 5

About the Speaking test

Part 1 (3 minutes)

In this part of the test, the examiner asks you and your partner some questions about yourselves. You may be asked questions about 'your family', 'your school', 'your free time', etc.

Part 2 (one-minute response from each candidate, plus a 20-second response from the second candidate)

In this part of the test, the examiner gives you two photos to talk about for one minute. The examiner then asks your partner a question about the photos and your partner responds briefly.

The examiner then gives two different photos to your partner to talk about. Afterwards, the examiner will ask you a question about your partner's photos and you respond briefly.

Part 3 (3 minutes)

In this part of the test, the examiner asks you and your partner to talk together. You may be asked to find a solution to a problem, or to decide something. For example, you may be asked to discuss the best place to visit on a school trip. The examiner gives you a picture with some ideas you can use, but does not join in the conversation.

Part 4 (4 minutes)

In this part of the test, the examiner asks you and your partner in turn some further questions in relation to what you have discussed in Part 3. You can also comment on your partner's answers.

Visual materials for Test 1

Why might the people choose to shop in these different places?

1A

1B

Visual materials for Test 1

> **Why do you think the people are wearing these different clothes?**

1C

1D

Visual materials for Test 1

- **Which of these jobs would you like to do?**
- **Which two jobs would be the best ways to earn a bit of extra money?**

1E

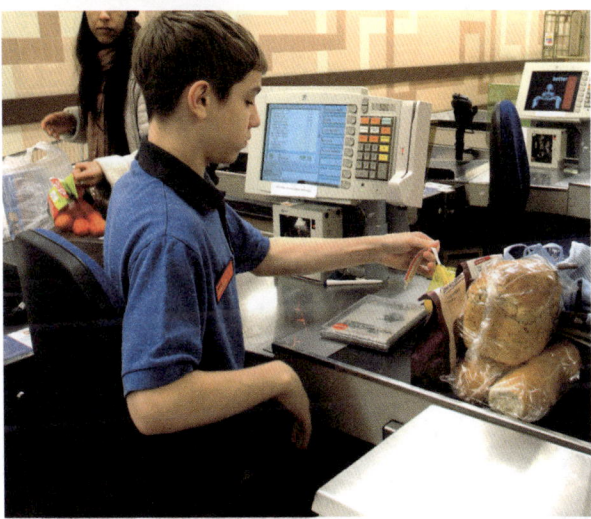

Visual materials for Test 2

> **Why do you think the people are giving these gifts?**

2A

2B

Visual materials for Test 2

> **What are the advantages and disadvantages of these styles of eating?**

2C

2D

Visual materials for Test 2

- **How suitable might these sports be for a sports competition with your class?**
- **Which two sports do you think would be best for your class?**

2E

Test 1
Paper 5 Examiner's script
Speaking Part 1 (3 minutes)

Good morning/afternoon/evening. My name is .... and this is my colleague ....

And your names are?

Can I have your mark sheets, please?

Thank you.

First of all we'd like to know something about you.

- Where are you from, *(Candidate A)*?
- And you, *(Candidate B)*?

- What do you like about living *(here/name of candidate's home town)*?
- And what about you, *(Candidate A/B)*?

Select one or more questions from any of the following categories, as appropriate.

The internet

- How often do you use the internet?
- Is it easy for you to use the internet? .... (Why?/Why not?)
- Do you need the internet to do your homework? .... (How often?)
- Do you use the internet to communicate with your friends? .... (Why?/Why not?)
- Would you find it easy to live without the internet? .... (Why?/Why not?)

Taking exercise

- Do you play any sports? .... (Which sports do you play?)
- Do you think it is important to take exercise? .... (Why?/Why not?)
- What do you think are the best forms of exercise? .... (Why?)
- What other things can you do to stay healthy? .... (Do you do these things?)
- What sports or types of exercise would you like to try? .... (Why?)

Speaking Part 2 (4 minutes)

| 1 Shopping |
| 2 Fashion |

Examiner	In this part of the test, I'm going to give each of you two photographs. I'd like you to talk about your photographs on your own for about a minute, and also to answer a short question about your partner's photographs.
	(*Candidate A*), it's your turn first. Here are your two photographs. They show **people shopping in different places**.
	*Give Candidate A photographs **1A** and **1B** (page 49).*
	I'd like you to compare the photographs, and say **why the people might choose to shop in these different places**.
	All right?
Candidate A *1 minute*	....
Examiner	Thank you. *Retrieve photographs.*
	(*Candidate B*), **how often do you go shopping**?
Candidate B *approximately 20 seconds*	....
Examiner	Thank you.
	Now, (*Candidate B*), here are your two photographs. They show **people wearing different types of clothes**.
	*Give Candidate B photographs **1C** and **1D** (page 50).*
	I'd like you to compare the photographs, and say **why you think the people are wearing these different clothes**.
	All right?
Candidate B *1 minute*	....
Examiner	Thank you. *Retrieve photographs.*
	(*Candidate A*), **which of these styles do you prefer**?
Candidate A *approximately 20 seconds*	....
Examiner	Thank you.

Speaking Parts 3 and 4 (7 minutes)

Earning money

Part 3

Examiner Now, I'd like you to talk about something together for about three minutes.

Here are some pictures of teenagers earning money in different ways at the weekend.

Place photographs 1E (page 51) *in front of the candidates.*

First talk to each other about **which of these jobs you would like to do**. Then decide **which two jobs would be the best ways to earn a bit of extra money**.

All right?

Candidates
3 minutes

....

Examiner Thank you. *Retrieve photographs.*

Part 4

Examiner *Select any of the following questions, as appropriate:*

Select any of the following prompts, as appropriate:
• **What do you think?**
• **Do you agree?**
• **And you?**

- **Have you ever done any of these jobs yourself?**

- **Did you enjoy it? (Why?/Why not?)**

- **What else do you think teenagers could do to earn some pocket money?**

- **Do you think parents should give their children pocket money? (Why?/Why not?)**

- **What do you think people learn by doing part-time or weekend jobs, or helping in the house to earn some money?**

- **Do you think children should help their parents in the house without expecting any money in return? (Why?/Why not?)**

Thank you. That is the end of the test.

Test 2
Paper 5 Examiner's script
Speaking Part 1 (3 minutes)

Good morning/afternoon/evening. My name is .... and this is my colleague ....

And your names are?

Can I have your mark sheets, please?

Thank you.

First of all we'd like to know something about you.

- Where are you from, (*Candidate A*)?
- And you, (*Candidate B*)?
- What do you like about living (*here/name of candidate's home town*)?
- And what about you, (*Candidate A/B*)?

Select one or more questions from any of the following categories, as appropriate.

School life

- Are there a lot of students at your school? .... (How many people are there in your class?)
- Do you live near your school? .... (How far do you live from school?)
- What do you like about your school?
- What is your favourite subject? .... (What do you like about it?)
- Did you go to another school before the one you attend now? .... (Was it very different?)

TV and films

- What kind of films do you enjoy watching? .... (What do you like about these kinds of films?)
- Who do you watch films with? .... (What do you think is good about watching films with other people?)
- What's the most recent film you have seen? .... (Why did/didn't you like it?)
- What do you think watching films adds to your life? .... (Why?)
- Do you prefer to watch films on a personal computer or on a larger screen? .... (Why?)

Speaking Part 2 (4 minutes)

1 Giving gifts
2 Food and drink

Examiner	In this part of the test, I'm going to give each of you two photographs. I'd like you to talk about your photographs on your own for about a minute, and also to answer a short question about your partner's photographs.
	(*Candidate A*), it's your turn first. Here are your two photographs. They show **people giving and receiving gifts**.
	Give Candidate A photographs 2A and 2B (page 52).
	I'd like you to compare the photographs, and say **why you think the people are giving these gifts**.
	All right?
Candidate A *1 minute*	....
Examiner	Thank you. *Retrieve photographs.*
	(*Candidate B*), **what kind of gift would you prefer to receive**?
Candidate B *approximately 20 seconds*	....
Examiner	Thank you.
	Now, (*Candidate B*), here are your two photographs. They show **people eating in different restaurants**.
	Give Candidate B photographs 2C and 2D (page 53).
	I'd like you to compare the photographs, and say **what you think the advantages and disadvantages are of these two styles of eating**.
	All right?
Candidate B *1 minute*	....
Examiner	Thank you. *Retrieve photographs.*
	(*Candidate A*), **where do you like to eat**?
Candidate A *approximately 20 seconds*	....
Examiner	Thank you.

Speaking Parts 3 and 4 (7 minutes)

Competitive sports

Part 3

Examiner	Now, I'd like you to talk about something together for about three minutes.
	Here are some pictures of different competitive sports.
	*Place photographs **2E** (page 54) in front of the candidates.*
	First talk to each other about **how suitable these sports might be for a sports competition with your class**. Then decide **which two sports you think would be best for your class**.
	All right?
Candidates *3 minutes*	....
Examiner	Thank you. *Retrieve photographs.*

Part 4

Examiner

Select any of the following questions, as appropriate:

- **Have you done any of these sports?**

- **Did you enjoy it? (Why?/Why not?)**

- **What other sports could a group of friends enjoy together?**

- **Do you think it's more fun to play competitive sports or non-competitive sports? (Why?)**

- **Do you prefer playing team sports or individual sports? (Why?)**

- **What are the advantages of playing competitive sports? (Why?)**

Select any of the following prompts, as appropriate:

- **What do you think?**
- **Do you agree?**
- **And you?**

Thank you. That is the end of the test.